APEX PREDATORS
of the Amazon Rain Forest

# Green Anaconda

## by Ellen Lawrence

**Consultant:**

**Stephen Hammack**
Herpetarium Keeper, St. Louis Zoo,
St. Louis, Missouri

BEARPORT PUBLISHING

New York, New York

**Credits**

Cover, © Arco Images GmbH/Alamy; 4, © Vadim Petrakov/Shutterstock; 5, © David Persson/Shutterstock; 6T, © Marcos Amend/Shutterstock; 6B, © Cosmographics; 7, © Sylvain Cordier/Biosphoto/FLPA; 8, © Pete Oxford/Minden Pictures/FLPA; 9, © M. Watson/Ardea; 10, © Claus Meyer/Minden Pictures/FLPA; 11, © Vladimir Wrangel/Shutterstock; 12, © chamleunejai/Shutterstock; 13, © Jean-Michel Labat/Ardea; 14T, © Pete Oxford/Minden Pictures/FLPA; 14B, © Mike Lane/Alamy; 15, © Francois Gohier/Ardea; 16, © M. Watson/Ardea; 17, © Creative Commons; 18, © age fotostock/Alamy; 19, © Ameet Zaveri; 20, © Tony Crocetta/Biosphoto; 21, © Vadim Petrakov/Shutterstock; 22, © Shutterstock and © Switlana Symonenko/Shutterstock; 23TL, © Claus Meyer/Minden Pictures/FLPA; 23TC, © M. Watson/Ardea; 23TR, © Patryk Kosmider/Shutterstock; 23BL, © Vadim Petrakov/Shutterstock; 23BC, © Filipe Frazao/Shutterstock; 23BR, © Jannarong/Shutterstock.

Publisher: Kenn Goin
Editor: Jessica Rudolph
Creative Director: Spencer Brinker
Photo Researcher: Ruby Tuesday Books Ltd

*Library of Congress Cataloging-in-Publication Data*

Names: Lawrence, Ellen, 1967– , author.
Title: Green anaconda / by Ellen Lawrence.
Description: New York, New York : Bearport Publishing, 2017. | Series: Apex predators of the Amazon rain forest | Includes bibliographical references and index. | Audience: Ages 5 to 8.
Identifiers: LCCN 2016043977 (print) | LCCN 2016050446 (ebook) | ISBN 9781684020317 (library) | ISBN 9781684020836 (book)
Subjects: LCSH: Anaconda—Juvenile literature.
Classification: LCC QL666.O63 .L39 2017 (print) | LCC QL666.O63 (ebook) | DDC 597.96/7—dc23
LC record available at https://lccn.loc.gov/2016043977

For more information, write to Bearport Publishing Company, Inc., 45 West 21st Street, Suite 3B, New York, New York 10010. Printed in the United States of America.

10 9 8 7 6 5 4 3 2 1

# Contents

# No Escape!

It's early evening in the Amazon **rain forest**.

A capybara slowly approaches a riverbank to take a drink.

The animal doesn't know it's being watched.

Suddenly, a green anaconda bursts out of the muddy water!

The capybara has no chance to escape from the giant, powerful **predator**.

capybara

The green anaconda is one of the largest snakes in the world. A female may grow to be 17 feet (5.2 m) long and weigh 200 pounds (91 kg). The male is much smaller but may be as long as 10 feet (3 m).

green anaconda

# A Green Anaconda's World

Green anacondas live in South America.

They often make their homes in rain forests, such as the Amazon, where slow-moving rivers flow beneath the trees.

Tangled plants grow at the edges of the rivers and float on the murky water.

The huge snakes swim and rest among the water plants.

a river in the Amazon rain forest

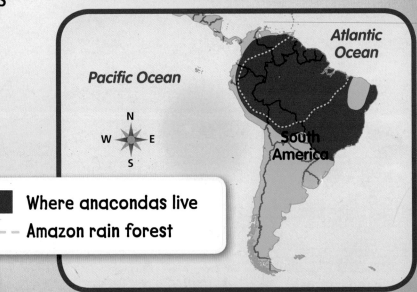

Atlantic Ocean

Pacific Ocean

South America

N
W — E
S

■ Where anacondas live
- - - Amazon rain forest

Snakes are a type of reptile. A reptile's body temperature changes when the air or water around it heats up or cools. Sometimes a green anaconda leaves the cool water to warm up in the sun's rays.

Imagine you are a scientist and you spot an anaconda in the Amazon. How would you describe the animal?

# Meet an Anaconda

A green anaconda has a thick, muscular body.

It has greenish-brown, **scaly** skin with a pattern of dark, egg-shaped spots.

An anaconda's eyes and nostrils are on the top of its head.

This allows the snake to see and breathe when it's swimming on the surface of a river.

How do you think the snake's color and pattern help it when it's hunting?

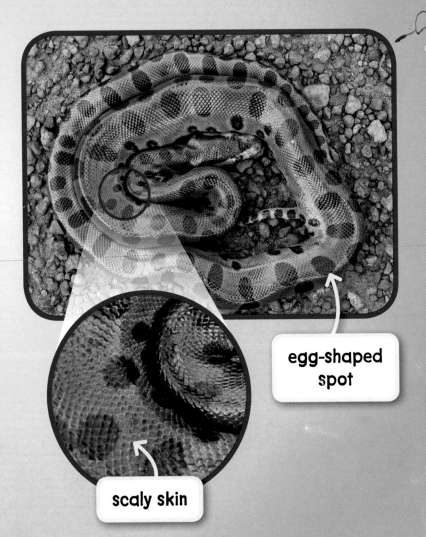

egg-shaped spot

scaly skin

# River Hunter

A green anaconda hunts by lurking in shallow water.

When an animal comes to the river to drink, it can't see the snake. Why?

The snake's skin color and pattern help it blend in with the plants and muddy water.

This **camouflage** allows the giant hunter to approach at high speed and grab its prey without being noticed.

an anaconda blending in with its surroundings

Sometimes an anaconda wraps itself around a tree branch hanging over a river. When the snake detects prey in the water, it slowly uncurls and lowers itself into the river to hunt.

an anaconda hunting in a river

What do you think the snake does after it grabs its prey?

# The Big Squeeze

After an anaconda bites its prey, it quickly coils its muscular body around the animal.

Then the snake squeezes its prey tighter and tighter.

It squeezes so hard that blood stops flowing through the animal's body.

Sometimes an animal drowns as it tries to struggle free.

Once the prey is dead, the anaconda swallows its meal—whole!

An anaconda is able to open its jaws very wide. It can swallow an animal much bigger than its own head!

an anaconda squeezing its prey

turtle

13

# A Large Meal

An adult anaconda can catch and swallow animals that are heavier than itself, such as deer, capybaras, and caimans.

An anaconda's skin stretches to allow a big meal to reach its stomach.

Sometimes a snake that has just eaten a large animal has a huge bump in its body!

red brocket deer

caiman

# Baby Anacondas

Anacondas usually live alone.

In spring, male and female snakes meet up and **mate**.

Seven months after mating, a female snake gives birth to about 30 babies.

The little anacondas are usually born in shallow water.

female anaconda

male

# Little Predators

A female anaconda doesn't take care of her babies.

The newborn snakes know how to look after themselves.

They hide among plants to stay safe from enemies, such as caimans and adult anacondas.

They swim in rivers and hunt for rats, fish, small lizards, and birds.

Just like their mother, the babies squeeze their prey to death!

a baby anaconda hunting

A newborn anaconda may be up to 3 feet (1 m) long. It weighs about half a pound (227 grams).

a scientist holding a baby anaconda

19

# An Amazon Giant

Adult green anacondas are top, or apex, predators in their Amazon home.

This means they hunt and eat their neighbors, but not many animals hunt them.

If a large caiman or jaguar attacks an anaconda, the powerful snake fights back.

Its enormous size helps the giant snake avoid becoming a meal!

green anaconda

caiman

an anaconda fighting with a caiman

As a snake grows, its scaly skin gets too tight. What do you think the snake does when this happens? (The answer is on page 24.)

Researchers holding a live adult green anaconda

Green anacondas keep growing their whole lives. They can live to be 30 years old.

# Science Lab

An adult female anaconda can grow to be 17 feet (5.2 m) long. Let's compare!

## Measure and Draw an Anaconda

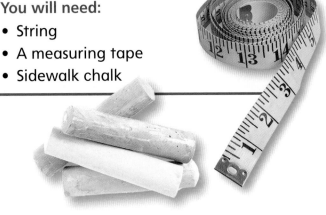

You will need:
- String
- A measuring tape
- Sidewalk chalk

1. Use a measuring tape to measure a piece of string that is 17 feet (5.2 m) long.

2. Stretch out the string and lay it on a playground. Ask some friends to lay head to toe alongside the string.

- *How many children fit into the length of a green anaconda?*

3. Now lay the string on the playground in a curvy shape, like a real snake. Draw a snake shape around the string.

- *Walk heel to toe alongside your snake. How many heel-to-toe footsteps fit into the anaconda?*

# Science Words

**camouflage** (KAM-uh-flahzh) patterns and colors on an animal's skin or fur that help it blend in with its surroundings

**mate** (MAYT) to come together to produce young

**predator** (PRED-uh-tur) an animal that hunts other animals for food

**prey** (PRAY) an animal that is hunted and eaten by another animal

**rain forest** (RAYN FORE-ist) a large area of land covered with trees and other plants where lots of rain falls

**scaly** (SKAYL-ee) having scales, which are small, tough, overlapping sections, or plates, on a reptile's skin

# Index

# Read More

Avery, Sebastian. *Anacondas (Snakes on the Hunt)*. New York: PowerKids Press (2017).

Goldish, Meish. *Reticulated Python: The World's Longest Snake (More SuperSized!)*. New York: Bearport (2010).

Smith, Molly. *Green Anaconda: The World's Heaviest Snake (SuperSized!)*. New York: Bearport (2007).

# Learn More Online

To learn more about green anacondas, visit **www.bearportpublishing.com/ApexPredators**

# About the Author

Ellen Lawrence lives in the United Kingdom. Her favorite books to write are those about nature and animals. In fact, the first book Ellen bought for herself, when she was six years old, was the story of a gorilla named Patty Cake that was born in New York's Central Park Zoo.

# Answer for Page 20

A snake sheds, or loses, its skin every few months. It wriggles out of the old, tight skin, and underneath is a new, bigger skin.